ADVANCED AND DUPLICATE BRIDGE STUDENT TEXT

Shirley Silverman

Revised by Pat Harrington and Harry Silverman

Published by
BARON BARCLAY BRIDGE SUPPLIES
1-800-274-2221

DEDICATION TO 1996 EDITION

This revised edition is dedicated to the memory of **Shirley Silverman**, who did so much to help students of the game of bridge find both enlightenment and enjoyment.

ACKNOWLEDGMENTS

The author wishes to thank Bill and Marietta Passell for their constructive suggestions and for putting at her disposal their encyclopedic knowledge of the game. Thanks are also due to Steve Becker of Greenwich, Conn. and Millie Washington of Poughkeepsie, N.Y. for help in organizing the duplicate section of this book, and to William Wise of Newtown Square, Pennsylvania, for editorial assistance.

Call, write or fax Baron Barclay Bridge Supplies for your free 64-page catalog of bridge books and supplies.

Third Printing March 1998

Baron Barclay Bridge Supplies
3600 Chamberlain Lane, Suite 230
Louisville, Kentucky 40241
1-800-274-2221
FAX 502-426-2044

Printed in U.S.A.

CONTENTS

Part I

Part II
DUPLICATE BRIDGE

EACH TRICK OVER SIX:

	SUITS			
	Club	Diamond	Heart	Spade
	20	20	30	30

If doubled, multiply by two; if redoubled, multiply by four.

NOTRUMP	
1st Trick	Each subsequent trick
40	30

OVERTRICKS:

	Not Vulnerable Trick Value	Vulnerable Trick Value
Undoubled, each..................		
Doubled, each.......................	100	200
Redoubled, each	200	400

SLAMS:

Small slam	500	750
Grand slam	1000	1500

HONORS
(If held in one hand)

Four honors	100
Five honors	150
Four aces at notrump	150

UNDERTRICKS:

	Not Vulnerable		Vulnerable	
	Undoubled	Doubled	Undoubled	Doubled
1st undertrick	50	100	100	200
Second and third undertricks	50	200	100	300
Each subsequent undertrick	50	300	100	300

If redoubled, multiply doubled value by two.

Premiums

Winning first two games: 700. Winning two out of three: 500.
Unfinished rubber (one game): 300
Winner of score in unfinished game: 100.
Making a doubled contract: 50.
Making a redoubled contract: 100.

INTRODUCTION

Bridge is a partnership game. When both partners are on the same wavelength playing becomes a pleasure. On the other hand, when you think a bid means one thing, and your partner thinks it means something else the result is seldom good.

In this text you will learn many new bids. They are only useful if both partners understand them. It is impossible in these few pages to go into all of the possible ramifications of these bids. If you wish to use them successfully, first discuss them with your partner, and then try them out. If a bid produces a bad result (and they occasionally will) discuss the problem with your partner AFTER THE GAME IS OVER.

* * *

If you like bridge, you should love duplicate bridge. Don't let the mechanics of the game or the supposed expertise of "experienced" duplicate players intimidate you. You probably already play better than fifty percent of those playing duplicate bridge regularly.

Once you have mastered duplicate, you will have a new hobby, one that knows no physical or territorial boundaries. Duplicate players range in age from 10 to 100, they play in all types of weather and in all corners of the world.

Join the American Contract Bridge League. As a member you are part of an organization of almost a quarter of a million bridge players, all dedicated to the enjoyment of their favorite game.

BRIDGE PROPRIETIES

An accepted code of bridge etiquette and bridge ethics has grown up during the centuries in which the game has been played. *There are no penalties for a breach of ethics.* Intentional violations of bridge proprieties are considered dishonest and ungentlemanly, but it is not within the scope of the bridge laws to penalize them.

DO NOT bid or play with special emphasis or use any inflection of the voice which would give partner information on the nature of your hand.

DO NOT watch the cards as they are being dealt; do not draw inferences about the place in his hand from which another player pulls a card in playing.

DO NOT express displeasure (or satisfaction) at a lead, play, bid, double or any other call partner makes.

DO NOT draw any inferences from the fact that partner has hesitated, or has bid with any special emphasis or inflection.

DO NOT hesitate, either in the bidding or in the play, in order to deceive the opponents.

DO NOT use any conventional bids known to you and partner which have not been explained to the opponents. The term *conventional bid* is any bid (or double or redouble) which has a special meaning to your partner not generally used by the other players at the table.

DO NOT prepare to lead to a trick before the previous trick is completed, or to take in a trick before it is completed, since this may inform partner as to cards in your hand.

DO NOT announce the score in order to call partner's attention to the fact that you have a partscore and a lower bid than usual will be enough for game.

BUT: It is not your duty to call attention to your side's breach of law, such as a revoke made by you or your partner.

LESSON ONE

Opening Weak Two Bids

OPENING WEAK TWO BIDS

Used only in spades, hearts, and diamonds
Fewer high card points than an opening one bid

In first or second seat
6 cards in bid suit
5 to 10 (or 11) high card points
Most of the strength in the bid suit
Usually 2 of the top 4 honors
Little defensive strength outside the bid suit
No outside 4-card major
Usually no void (a void can make your hand too good)

In third seat
Bid suit may be very strong 5-card or weak 7-card suit
May have more outside strength
May have outside weak 4-card major
May have a void

In fourth seat
Good 6-card suit
9-12 high card points
Bid only if you expect a positive score (you expect you
    can make your bid and the opponents are unlikely
    to be able to successfully outbid you).

Vulnerability
Vulnerable preempts are more dangerous because of
    the risk of being doubled.
Must have a good suit when vulnerable (honors and high
    spot cards — 10, 9, 8)

Assume that you are opening weak two bids. What is the correct opening bid with each of the following hands in first or second seat?

(1) ♠ A Q J 8 7 5   (2) ♠ K Q J 8 7 5   (3) ♠ K Q J 8 7 5
   ♥ 9 7 4   ♥ 10   ♥ K 9 8 4
   ♦ 9 7 6   ♦ K 9 8 4   ♦ 8 7
   ♣ 5   ♣ 7 2   ♣ 10

(1)_____   (2)_____   (3)_____

(4) ♠ K Q J 9 8 7   (5) ♠ 8 7   (6) ♠ K J 5 4 3 2
   ♥ 8 4   ♥ A Q J 8 7 5   ♥ 9 8
   ♦ 9 8 5   ♦ 8 2   ♦ Q 7 5
   ♣ 8 3   ♣ K 5 4   ♣ 9 5

(4)_____   (5)_____   (6)_____

(1) 2♠. (2) 2♠. (3) Pass; hearts might be a better trump suit. (4) 2♠. (5) 2♥. (6) Pass if vulnerable; this is *not* a good suit. Daring bidders might venture a non-vulnerable 2♠ bid.

Playing weak two bids, what is the correct opening bid with each of the following hands in third seat?

(7) ♠ A K J 8 7   (8) ♠ K Q J 8 6 4   (9) ♠ Q J 10 8 6 3
   ♥ 5   ♥ 8 7 4 2   ♥ 7
   ♦ Q 8 4 3   ♦ 8 4   ♦ K 7 3
   ♣ 9 8 2   ♣ 10   ♣ K 5 2

(7)_____   (8)_____   (9)_____

(10) ♠ A K Q J 9   (11) ♠ Q 8 7   (12) ♠ 9 7 6
    ♥ 9 4   ♥ A Q J 10 6 2   ♥ 9
    ♦ 9 8 6 4 3   ♦ 8 6 4 2   ♦ K 7 5
    ♣ 9   ♣ —   ♣ Q J 10 9 4 3

(10)_____   (11)_____   (12)_____

(7) 2♠. (8) 2♠; you aren't risking missing a heart game when partner has passed. (9) 2♠. (10) 2♠. (11) 2♥. (12) Pass; two clubs is not a weak bid – see Lesson Two.

8

Playing weak two bids, what is the correct opening bid with each of the following hands in fourth seat?

(13) ♠ A K J 8 7 5
    ♥ 9
    ♦ 8 6 4
    ♣ K 9 5

(14) ♠ A K J 8 7 3
    ♥ 7
    ♦ 9 3 2
    ♣ A 5 4

(15) ♠ A 5
    ♥ 6 4
    ♦ K J 9 8 7 4
    ♣ J 7 6

(13)_____   (14)_____   (15)_____

(13) 2♠. (14) 2♠. (15) Pass; there's too much danger of opening to let the opponents make a major suit contract.

RESPONSES TO OPENING WEAK TWO BIDS

Weak hands:
  Pass with a poor fit.
  Further the preempt with a good fit. *need extra*
    Bid 3 of partner's suit with 3 trumps. *points beside*
    Bid 4 of partner's suit with 4 trumps. *trumps.*
    Raise 2♦ to game with 5 trumps.
  The opening preemptive bidder must not bid again after responder raises.

Good hand (16 points and about 5 quick tricks, not queens and jacks):
  Bid game in partner's suit with a fit and 5 quick tricks.
  Bid 3NT with 9 playing tricks in your own hand or with stoppers in all suits and a good fit for partner's suit (usually diamonds).
  The bid of a new suit by responder who has never passed is normally forcing and shows a long suit. By a passed hand, it usually shows a long suit with no support for partner. Each partnership must discuss these options.
  Bid 2NT (forcing) to request more information. By partnership agreement, 2NT is either asking for a feature or Ogust.

```
┌─────────────────────────────────────────────────────────┐
│              2NT ASKING FOR A FEATURE                   │
│                                                         │
│                 To get more information,                │
│            partner of weak two bidder bids 2NT.         │
│                                                         │
│  With a maximum, opener shows an outside feature        │
│    (A or K).                                            │
│  With a minimum, opener rebids his suit on the three level. │
│  With a solid suit (AKQxxx or better), opener rebids 3NT. │
└─────────────────────────────────────────────────────────┘
```

The bidding has gone as follows:

PARTNER	OPPONENT	YOU
2♠ (weak)	Pass	?

(16) ♠ 8 6
    ♥ A 7 2
    ♦ 8 5 4 2
    ♣ K J 7 6

(17) ♠ Q 9 4 3
    ♥ 9
    ♦ K J 7 6 4
    ♣ 9 4 2

(18) ♠ K 9 4
    ♥ 4 2
    ♦ A 9 7 6
    ♣ 9 8 5 2

(16)_____　　(17)_____　　(18)_____

(19) ♠ K 7 2
    ♥ A K
    ♦ A Q J 8 4 3
    ♣ 7 6

(20) ♠ —
    ♥ A Q 2
    ♦ A K Q J 7 6 2
    ♣ K Q 9

(21) ♠ K 7 4
    ♥ A K 2
    ♦ Q J 9
    ♣ Q J 5 4

(19)_____　　(20)_____　　(21)_____

(22) ♠ K 5 3
    ♥ A
    ♦ A Q J 9 7 3
    ♣ A Q 3

(23) ♠ 10
    ♥ K Q J 8 7 2
    ♦ 7 6 4 2
    ♣ 6 4

(24) ♠ A 7 4 3
    ♥ 7 6 2
    ♦ 8 6 5 3 2
    ♣ 8

(22)_____　　(23)_____　　(24)_____

(16) **Pass**. (17) 4♠ (as a preempt to help shut out a four heart bid). (18) 3♠. (19) 4♣ (to make). (20) 3NT. (21) 2NT (forcing). You will stop in 3♠ if partner shows a minimum weak two but will bid game if partner shows a good weak two. (22) 2NT (forcing). If partner shows a minor suit feature, you can consider bidding a slam. (23) **Pass**. (24) 4♠ — the opponents must be able to make game or even slam.

The bidding has gone:

YOU	OPPONENT	PARTNER	OPPONENT
Pass	Pass	2♠ (weak)	Double
?			

What should you bid with each of these hands?

(25) ♠ 8 6 4 3
    ♥ 7
    ♦ A 8 7 4 3
    ♣ 9 8 5

(26) ♠ 8 4
    ♥ 9 6 5 3
    ♦ 9 8 4 2
    ♣ A K Q

(27) ♠ —
    ♥ A 8 7 6 4
    ♦ 7 4 3 2
    ♣ K Q J 5

(25)_____   (26)_____   (27)_____

(25) 4♠; make it hard for doubler's partner to uncover the heart fit. (26) Pass. (27) Don't look troubled; just pass. The double is for takeout; there's a good chance that the opponents will bid one of your suits.

Rather than use a 2NT response to ask the weak two bidder for a feature, some players prefer the Ogust Convention. If you decide to use Ogust, 2NT asks the weak two bidder to further describe his hand as follows:

OGUST CONVENTION		
OPENER 2♦/2♥/2♠	**OPPONENT** Pass	**RESPONDER** 2NT
OPENER'S REBID	**STRENGTH OF HAND**	**QUALITY OF SUIT**
3♣	minimum	bad
3♦	minimum	good
3♥	maximum	bad
3♠	maximum	good
3NT	maximum	solid suit

It is easy to remember the meaning of the opener's rebids — just keep in mind that the description of the *hand* comes before the description of the *suit*.

A minimum hand is at the lower end of the weak two point range (5-8 HCP). A maximum hand is at the upper end of the range (9-11 HCP).

A good suit has at least two of the top three honors plus good spot cards —

A Q J 7 5 4	A Q 10 9 8 5
A K 10 9 7 5	K Q J 8 6 5

A bad suit has fewer honors and spot cards —

A Q 5 4 3 2	K J 9 6 5 4
Q J 10 7 6 5	K Q 6 4 3 2

The bidding has gone as follows. What is the correct rebid with each hand?

YOU	OPPONENT	PARTNER	OPPONENT
2♠	Pass	2NT	Pass
?			

(28) ♠ Q J 8 4 3 2
♥ 7
♦ K Q J
♣ 7 5 2

(29) ♠ A Q J 10 9 4
♥ 2
♦ 9 4 2
♣ K 8 3

(30) ♠ A K J 8 6 3
♥ 8 4
♦ 8 3
♣ 7 6 5

(28)_____ (29)_____ (30)_____

(31) ♠ A K Q 9 8 7
♥ 9
♦ 9 7 3
♣ 8 3 2

(32) ♠ K J 8 7 5 4
♥ 7 6 2
♦ K Q J
♣ 8

(33) ♠ K J 10 8 7 6
♥ 9 8
♦ K 6 3
♣ 10 7

(31)_____ (32)_____ (33)_____

Using "feature" responses: (28) 3♦. (29) 3♣. (30) 3♠. (31) 3NT. (32) 3♦. (33) 3♠. Don't show a feature with a minimum hand.

Using Ogust responses: (28) 3♥. (29) 3♠. (30) 3♣. (31) 3NT. (32) 3♠. (33) 3♣.

LESSON TWO

Opening Notrump Bids
Strong Two Club Opening

Using weak two bids, a two club opening is used for all strong hands regardless of suit. A strong two club opening is forcing to two notrump, three of a major or game, by partnership agreement.

STRONG TWO CLUB OPENING
Forcing to 2NT, 3 of a major or game
by partnership agreement

Many players who use the strong two club bid open one notrump with 15-17 points instead of the traditional 16-18 points. Changing the opening range has little effect on responses. A good 8-9 point hand will still invite game with two notrump or Stayman. With a good 10 or more points, it's responder's job to see that game is reached. Changing to a 15-17 point one notrump opening has an effect on other notrump opening bids and rebids.

BIDDING WITH BALANCED HANDS

Using 15-17 1NT openings		Using 16-18 1NT openings
12-14 points	open a suit; can rebid 1NT	13-15 points
15-17 points	open 1NT	16-18 points
18-19 points	open a suit; can rebid 2NT (highly invitational)	19-20 points
20-21 points	open 2NT	21-22 points
22-24 points	open 2♣; rebid 2NT	23-24 points
25-27 points	open 2♣; rebid 3NT	25-27 points

You are using two clubs as a strong forcing opening bid. What is the correct opening bid with each of these hands?

(1)
♠ 8
♥ A Q J 7 4
♦ A K Q
♣ A Q J 8

(1)_____

(2)
♠ A Q 7
♥ K 9 7 2
♦ A Q J 7
♣ A J

(2)_____

(3)
♠ A K 8
♥ A Q
♦ K Q J 6
♣ A J 7 3

(3)_____

(4)
♠ A Q J 7 5 2
♥ K Q J 8 7
♦ A
♣ A

(4)_____

(5)
♠ A Q
♥ K Q J 9
♦ A Q J
♣ K Q J 6

(5)_____

(6)
♠ 8 5
♥ Q 7
♦ A K Q J 10 8 3
♣ 8 3

(6)_____

(1) 2♣. (2) 2NT. (3) 2♣. (4) 2♣. (5) 2♣. (6) 3NT.

The bidding has gone as follows: What do you respond with each of these hands?

PARTNER	OPPONENT	YOU
2♣	Pass	?

(7) ♠ Q 7 6
    ♥ 8 5 3
    ♦ 9 4
    ♣ 9 8 5 4 3

(8) ♠ A 8
    ♥ Q 7 6
    ♦ 10 8 7 2
    ♣ K 7 5 2

(9) ♠ A Q 8 7 4 3
    ♥ 9
    ♦ 8 6 4
    ♣ J 9 6

(7)_____   (8)_____   (9)_____

(7) 2♦. (8) 2NT. (9) 2♠.

The bidding has gone as follows. What do you rebid with each of these hands? Is your bid forcing?

YOU	OPPONENT	PARTNER	OPPONENT
2♣	Pass	2♦	Pass
?			

(10) ♠ 8
    ♥ A Q J 7 2
    ♦ A K Q
    ♣ A Q J 7

(11) ♠ A K 7
    ♥ A Q
    ♦ K Q J 10
    ♣ A J 8 7

(12) ♠ A Q J 8 4 3
    ♥ K Q J 8 6
    ♦ A
    ♣ A

(10)_____,_____   (11)_____,_____   (12)_____,_____

(13) ♠ A K
    ♥ K Q J 6
    ♦ A Q J
    ♣ K Q J 7

(14) ♠ A Q 7 4 2
    ♥ A
    ♦ K Q J 10 5
    ♣ A K

(15) ♠ A
    ♥ A K Q J 6 4
    ♦ A Q J 7 6 3
    ♣ —

(13)_____,_____   (14)_____,_____   (15)_____,_____

(16) ♠ A K Q J 7 6 3
    ♥ 8 5
    ♦ A K
    ♣ A Q

(17) ♠ A Q
    ♥ K Q
    ♦ A K J 8 5 4 3 2
    ♣ A

(18) ♠ Q J 9 2
    ♥ A K 10 7
    ♦ A K Q
    ♣ A K

(16)_____,_____   (17)_____,_____   (18)_____,_____

(10) 2♥, yes. (11) 2NT, no. (12) 2♠, Yes. (13) 3NT, no.
(14) 2♦, yes. (15) 2♥, yes. (16) 2♠, yes. (17) 3♦, yes.
(18) 3NT, no.

LESSON THREE

One Notrump Response
Forcing One Round

ONE NOTRUMP FORCING ONE ROUND
AFTER MAJOR SUIT OPENING

OPENER	RESPONDER
1♥/1♠	1NT (1NT forcing is used with
?	hands ranging from
	6 to 12 points.)

OPENER:
1. Rebids six card suit
2. Bids four card suit
3. Bids lower three card minor
4. Raises notrump with 18-19 points.

Most partnerships agree that 1NT is not a forcing bid when responder is a passed hand.

1NT forcing is not used in a competitive auction: 1♥ — 1♠ overcall — 1NT (not forcing).

SEQUENCES USED WHEN
PLAYING FORCING NOTRUMP

1♠	1NT
2♠ (minimum; 6-card suit)	

1♠	1NT
3♠ (medium; 6-card suit)	

1♥	1NT
2♥ (minimum; normally 6-card suit may be 5-card suit with 4-5-2-2 distribution)	

1♠	1NT
2♣ or 2♦ (may be 3-card minor; non-forcing)	

1♠	1NT
2NT (18-19 points)	

1♠	1NT
2♦	2♠ (weak hand with doubleton spade)

1♠	1NT
2♦	2♥ (weak hand with long heart suit; opener usually passes)

1♠	1NT
2 of any suit	2NT (10-12 points invitational)

1♠	1NT
2♥	3♠ (10-12 points; 3 trumps; invitational)

1♠	1NT
2♣	3 of a new suit — to play weak, very long suit, no spade support

You are playing a one notrump forcing response to a major suit opening. What is the proper response with each of the following hands, if your partner opens with one spade?

(1) ♠ 10 8
    ♥ Q 7 2
    ♦ A 9 7 4 3 2
    ♣ 7 4

(2) ♠ 7 5
    ♥ 8
    ♦ Q J 7 5 2
    ♣ K J 8 7 3

(3) ♠ 8
    ♥ A Q 9 8 7 5 3
    ♦ 10 8 6 3
    ♣ 10

(1)_____   (2)_____   (2)_____

(4) ♠ Q 6
    ♥ A Q 8 7
    ♦ 9 8 3 2
    ♣ K 7 6

(5) ♠ 8
    ♥ 7 5 3
    ♦ 8 3
    ♣ A J 9 8 5 3 2

(6) ♠ Q 8 3
    ♥ A J 4
    ♦ 9 8 6 3 2
    ♣ K 4

(4)_____   (5)_____   (6)_____

(1) 1NT. (2) 1NT. (3) 1NT. (4) 1NT. (5) 1NT. (6) 1NT.

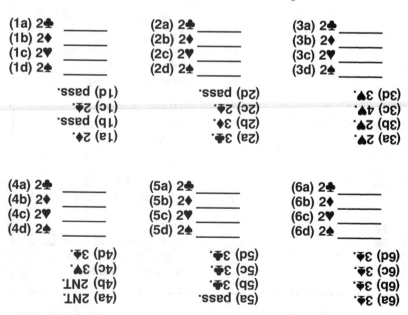

What is your next rebid with each hand if partner rebids:

(1a) 2♣ _____
(1b) 2♦ _____
(1c) 2♥ _____
(1d) 2♠ _____

(2a) 2♣ _____
(2b) 2♦ _____
(2c) 2♥ _____
(2d) 2♠ _____

(3a) 2♣ _____
(3b) 2♦ _____
(3c) 2♥ _____
(3d) 2♠ _____

(1a) 2♦.
(1b) pass.
(1c) 2♠.
(1d) pass.

(2a) 3♣.
(2b) 3♦.
(2c) 2♦.
(2d) pass.

(3a) 2♥.
(3b) 2♥.
(3c) 4♥.
(3d) 3♥.

(4a) 2♣ _____
(4b) 2♦ _____
(4c) 2♥ _____
(4d) 2♠ _____

(5a) 2♣ _____
(5b) 2♦ _____
(5c) 2♥ _____
(5d) 2♠ _____

(6a) 2♣ _____
(6b) 2♦ _____
(6c) 2♥ _____
(6d) 2♠ _____

(4a) 2NT.
(4b) 2NT.
(4c) 3♥.
(4d) 3♣.

(5a) pass.
(5b) 3♣.
(5c) 3♣.
(5d) 3♣.

(6a) 3♣.
(6b) 3♣.
(6c) 3♣.
(6d) 3♣.

What do you rebid with each of these hands after partner has responded with a forcing notrump?

YOU	PARTNER
1♠	1NT

(7) ♠ A Q 9 8 3
♥ K 7
♦ 9 8 5 4
♣ A 9

(8) ♠ Q 9 7 5 3
♥ K J 8 3
♦ A 10
♣ A 8

(9) ♠ A K J 8 5 2
♥ 8 7
♦ J 7
♣ A 7 4

(7)_____

(8)_____

(9)_____

(10) ♠ A 7 4 3 2
♥ K J 9
♦ A Q 7
♣ A 8

(11) ♠ A J 8 7 6 5
♥ 10
♦ A Q 7 5 3
♣ 10

(12) ♠ A Q 9 8 7
♥ 9 8 7
♦ A K 9
♣ 9 8

(10)_____

(11)_____

(12)_____

(7) 2♦. (8) 2♥. (9) 2♠. (10) 2NT. (11) 2♦. (12) 2♦.

LESSON FOUR

Unusual Notrump — Michaels Cuebid

THE UNUSUAL NOTRUMP

A jump in notrump as your side's first bid or the cheapest
  notrump bid by a passed hand shows both minor suits.
Distribution: 5 clubs and 5 diamonds or better
  with most of your strength in the minors.
If vulnerable, shows a better hand or better distribution.

Examples:

OPPONENT	YOU	OPPONENT	PARTNER
1♠	2NT (unusual)		

OR

OPPONENT	YOU	OPPONENT	PARTNER
1♥	Pass	1♠	2NT (unusual)

OR

OPPONENT	YOU	OPPONENT	PARTNER
	Pass	1♥	Pass
1♠	1NT (unusual)		

OR

OPPONENT	YOU	OPPONENT	PARTNER
	Pass	1♠	2NT (unusual)

EXCEPTION

OPPONENT	YOU	OPPONENT	PARTNER
	Pass	1♥	Pass
Pass	1NT*		

*This is *not* the unusual notrump; it merely shows 11 or
12 balanced points and a stopper in opponent's suit.

Some players use the unusual notrump to show 5-5 distribution in
the two lower *unbid* suits.
Thus: 2NT after a 1♣ opening shows ♦ and ♥.
  2NT after a 1♦ opening shows ♣ and ♥.
Each partnership must decide whether to use the unusual notrump
to show only the minors or to show the two lower *unbid* suits.

Your right hand opponent opens the bidding with one heart. What should you bid with each of these hands, if you are using the unusual notrump convention?

(1)	♠ 84	(2)	♠ K8	(3)	♠ AQ7	(4)	♠ AK8
	♥ 9		♥ A		♥ —		♥ K43
	♦ AQ874		♦ K9643		♦ AJ1076		♦ AQ92
	♣ KJ1084		♣ 109876		♣ A7432		♠ AQ3

(1)_____   (2)_____   (3)_____   (4)_____

(1) 2NT. (2) Pass — your points should be in the suits you are showing. (3) Double. You have good holdings in both minors, but your spades would offer good support if this is partner's long suit. (4) Double. Since a two notrump bid would show a minor suit oriented hand, a strong notrump hand must be shown by doubling first and then bidding notrump.

Playing the unusual notrump convention, what should you bid with each of the following hands, when the bidding has gone as shown below:

OPPONENT	PARTNER	OPPONENT	YOU
1♥	2NT	Pass	?

(5)	♠ A 9 7	(6)	♠ A Q 8 4	(7)	♠ Q 7 6 4 3
	♥ 7 5 3		♥ 8 7 6 2		♥ 9 7 3 2
	♦ K 10 9 4		♦ 7 6		♦ 10 9
	♣ 8 7 3		♣ 7 5 3		♣ 8 6

(5)_____   (6)_____   (7)_____

(8)	♠ A Q 8 7 5 2	(9)	♠ 8	(10)	♠ A K Q
	♥ 9		♥ A 6 3		♥ A K Q
	♦ 9 7 4		♦ K J 3		♦ 9 7 6 3
	♣ 9 8 4		♣ A Q J 7 4 3		♣ 7 5 4

(8)_____   (9)_____   (10)_____

(5) 3♦. (6) 3♣. (7) 3♣. (8) 3♠. (9) 5♣ or 4NT (Blackwood). A slam is likely if partner has an ace. (10) 3NT.

THE MICHAELS CUEBID

An overcall in the opener's suit is a cuebid showing a two-suited hand.

A cuebid of a minor suit shows the majors — at least 5 hearts and 5 spades.

A cuebid of a major suit shows the other major and one of minors (at least 5-5).

Michaels may be used with any strength hand but many pairs prefer to use it only with weak hands or with strong hands; they overcall with sound opening hands. When bidding a weak hand, pay attention to vulnerability.

OPPONENT	YOU	
1♣	2♣	promises 5 hearts and 5 spades
1♦	2♦	promises 5 hearts and 5 spades
1♥	2♥	promises 5 spades and either 5 clubs or 5 diamonds
1♠	2♠	promises 5 hearts and either 5 clubs or 5 diamonds

AFTER PARTNER USES MICHAELS

For the majors:
  Without a fit make the cheapest bid in your longer major; pass if RHO bids first.
  With a fit and a good hand: bid the full value of your hand in your best major.
  With a good fit and a weak hand: consider making a sacrifice bid.

For a major and a minor:
  Bid as above with a fit for partner's major.
  Bid 2NT to ask for partner's minor suit.

Your right-hand opponent opened one diamond. You are not vulnerable. What action would you take with each of the following hands?

(11) ♠ KJ1075
    ♥ KQ987
    ♦ 9
    ♣ 87

(12) ♠ 97432
    ♥ J6542
    ♦ KQ
    ♣ A

(13) ♠ AK985
    ♥ KQ64
    ♦ 97
    ♣ 74

(14) ♠ AQJ96
    ♥ KQ983
    ♦ 5
    ♣ AQ

(11)_____   (12)_____   (13)_____   (14)_____

(15) ♠ A97542
    ♥ KJ987
    ♦ 3
    ♣ 6

(16) ♠ AQ1097
    ♥ K9654
    ♦ 2
    ♣ A5

(17) ♠ 976542
    ♥ K97432
    ♦ —
    ♣ 8

(15)_____   (16)_____   (17)_____

(11) 2♦. (12) Pass. Michaels is best used when most of your strength is in your long suits. (13) 1♠. You don't have the 5-5 distribution suggested for Michaels. There are some pairs who use Michaels with 5-4 distribution, but we don't recommend it. (14) 2♣. You will take another bid to let partner know that you have a strong hand rather than the usual weak hand. (15) 2♦. (16) 1♥. Sound opening hands are best shown by starting with an overcall. If the opponents' bidding goes slowly, you can bid hearts next time. The problem with a cuebid is that you will want to bid again. But, when you bid again, partner will expect more strength. (17) 2♦

You and partner have agreed to use Michaels. You are not vulnerable. What is your bid on each of the following hands after:

OPPONENT	PARTNER	OPPONENT	YOU
1♣	2♣	Pass	?

(18) ♠ 976
    ♥ 54
    ♦ J986
    ♣ 8743

(19) ♠ K975
    ♥ K7
    ♦ AQ6
    ♣ A742

(20) ♠ 7
    ♥ 53
    ♦ AJ763
    ♣ 97432

(21) ♠ 82
    ♥ K9752
    ♦ K6542
    ♣ 4

(18)_____   (19)_____   (20)_____   (21)_____

(18) 2♣. (Pass if your right-hand opponent bids.) (19) 4♣. (20) 2♦. You probably do not have an eight-card fit; hearts is your best trump suit. (21) 4♥. With so many hearts, preempt to make the opponents' bidding difficult.

You and partner have agreed to use Michaels. You are not vulnerable. How will you bid with the following hands after:

OPPONENT	PARTNER	OPPONENT	YOU
1♥	2♥	Pass	?

(22) ♠ 762
♥ 5432
♦ J983
♣ 92

(23) ♠ 5
♥ J72
♦ K973
♣ 109742

(24) ♠ 3
♥ J9762
♦ K742
♣ Q93

(25) ♠ 65
♥ AK42
♦ KJ942
♣ 92

(22)_____ (23)_____ (24)_____ (25)_____

(22) 2♣. (23) 2NT. Ask partner to show his minor suit. (24) 2NT; pass when partner shows his minor. (25) 2♣. Partner's minor is probably clubs. Stay low on misfit hands.

VULNERABILITY AND TWO-SUITED BIDS

Michaels and the Unusual Notrump are primarily used as preemptive bids. They may alert your partner to a good sacrifice over the opponents' game or partscore. Because they are sacrifice-oriented, the use of these bids depends on vulnerability. The best time for a sacrifice is when your side is not vulnerable and the opponents are vulnerable (known as favorable vulnerability). The worst time for a sacrifice is when you are vulnerable and the opponents are not (unfavorable vulnerability). Your opponents won't mind your stealing their game if they can double you and score better than they would for making a game!

EVALUATING YOUR HAND AFTER A TWO-SUITED BID

If partner makes a conventional bid to show two suits:
Remember that partner may be preempting rather than showing strength.
With a weak hand and a good fit for one of partner's suits, further the preempt.
With a stronger hand, look at *where* your points are. A good hand has points in partner's suits. Lower-ranking honors in the opponents' suits will not be useful. Bid game if you think you can make it.
If the two-suited bidder bids again, he shows a good hand (not a preempt).

LESSON FIVE

Drury

THE DRURY CONVENTION

(to keep a partnership at the two level when opener may have opened light in third or fourth seat).

A 2♣ response to a major suit opening by a passed hand shows 10 to 12 points and good support for partner's major.

YOU	OPPONENT	PARTNER	OPPONENT
Pass	Pass	1♥/1♠ *3rd chair majors only*	Pass
2♣ (Drury)			

The 2♣ Drury response asks opener to clarify his strength.

2♦ rebid by opener	=	a sub-minimum or a very bad minimum opener (responder goes back to two of the major)
Any other rebid by opener	=	a full opening hand with game interest

A positive response to a Drury bid requires another bid from responder.

YOU	OPPONENT	PARTNER	OPPONENT
Pass	Pass	1♠	Pass
2♣ (Drury) (must bid again)	Pass	2♠	Pass

Many players use Reverse Drury — opener's rebids over 2♣ are reversed.

2 of opener's major = sub-minimum or very bad minimum (responder will pass)
2 of any other suit = a full opening hand with game interest (responder must bid again)

What do you bid with each of these hands, if you are using the Drury convention? The bidding has gone as shown.

YOU	OPPONENT	PARTNER	OPPONENT
Pass	Pass	1♥	Pass
?			

(1) ♠ A 8 7
♥ K J 9 7
♦ Q J 7
♣ 4 3 2

(2) ♠ 6 3
♥ K J 8 7 3
♦ 8 7 4 3
♣ A Q

(3) ♠ A 7 6
♥ K 8 7 6
♦ 10 6 4
♣ A 8 7

(1)_____   (2)_____   (2)_____

(1) 2♣. (2) 2♣. (3) 2♣.

What do you rebid with each of the following hands? (The two club response is Drury.)

PARTNER	OPPONENT	YOU	OPPONENT
Pass	Pass	1♥	Pass
2♣	Pass	?	

(4) ♠ A 8 6
♥ K J 8 7 5
♦ K 7 6
♣ 8 7

(5) ♠ A K 7
♥ Q J 7 4 3
♦ A 9 8
♣ 6 5

(6) ♠ A
♥ K Q 7 4 3 2
♦ A J 8 7
♣ 4 3

(4)_____   (5)_____   (6)_____

(4) 2♦. (5) 2♥. (6) 2♠.

What do you rebid with each of the following hands? (The two club response is Drury.)

YOU	OPPONENT	PARTNER	OPPONENT
Pass	Pass	1♠	Pass
2♣	Pass	2♥	Pass
?			

(7) ♠ A 6 2
♥ K J 9 8
♦ K 3
♣ 10 8 7 2

(8) ♠ 10 6 5
♥ K Q
♦ A 7 6 3 2
♣ Q 5 2

(9) ♠ Q 5 4 2
♥ A Q
♦ K 9 8 7 3
♣ 7 5

(7)_____   (8)_____   (9)_____

(7) 4♥, showing a hand with four hearts and three spades.
(8) 2♠. (9) 4♥.

26

LESSON SIX
Notrump Conventions:
Jacoby, Texas, Landy, Brozel,
Cappelletti, Lebensohl

JACOBY TRANSFER BIDS
(in response to a one notrump opening)

**Enables the strong hand
to be concealed and receive the opening lead**

RESPONDER
2♣ Stayman
2♦ demands 2♥
2♥ demands 2♠

RESPONDER'S REBIDS AFTER RELAY

Pass	Weak one suited hand
2NT*	Game invitation
3♥/3♠	Game invitation; 6+ card suit
3NT*	Partner passes or bids game in suit.
	*Shows five cards in relay suit.
4♥/4♠	6+ card suit

(Jacoby can also be used after a two notrump opening.)

ADVANCED JACOBY TRANSFERS
(Decide with partner which to use)

2♠ demands better minor.
OR
2♠ demands 3♣.
2NT demands 3♦.*
OR
2♠ demands 3♣.
3♣ demands 3♦.

*If 2NT demands 3♦, responder must use a 2♠ response to
show 8-9 points and invite a bid of 3NT.

OPENER	RESPONDER
1NT	2♣ (does not guarantee four-card major)
2♣/♥/♠	2NT (shows 8 or 9 points)

Playing the Jacoby transfer convention, what do you bid with each of the following hands, after partner has opened with one notrump?

(1)
♠ A Q 8 7 5
♥ 9 8 7
♦ K Q 8
♣ 9 8

(2)
♠ 8
♥ K Q 8 7 5 4
♦ 8 7 3
♣ 8 6 4

(3)
♠ K J 7 6 5 2
♥ 9
♦ A 8 4
♣ K 10 9

(1)_____

(2)_____

(2)_____

(1) 2♥. (2) 2♦. (3) 2♥.

After partner makes the required rebid, what should you bid next?

(1a)_____

(2a)_____

(2a)_____

(1a) 3NT. (2a) pass. (3a) 4♣.

After the following sequence of bidding, what action should you take with each of the following hands?

YOU	OPPONENT	PARTNER	OPPONENT
1NT	Pass	2♥	Pass
2♠	Pass	3NT	Pass
?			

(4)
♠ A Q 8 7
♥ A 7 4
♦ K Q 8 4
♣ Q 7

(5)
♠ Q 5
♥ A J 10 5
♦ K Q 9 5
♣ A J 9

(6)
♠ A 8 6
♥ J 7 3
♦ A Q 8 5
♣ K Q 6

(4)_____

(5)_____

(6)_____

(4) 4♣. (5) Pass. (6) 4♣.

28

The bidding has gone as follows, playing Jacoby transfers. What should you do next?

YOU	OPPONENT	PARTNER	OPPONENT
1NT	Pass	2♦	Pass
2♥	Pass	2NT	Pass
?			

(7) ♠ A 8 7
♥ K 9
♦ A Q 5 4
♣ K 7 5 3

(8) ♠ K Q 5
♥ A 8
♦ K J 9 3
♣ A 10 5 3

(9) ♠ A 7 5
♥ K J 7 6
♦ A 8
♣ A J 9 2

(7)_____ (8)_____ (9)_____

(7) Pass. (8) 3NT. (9) 4♥.

The bidding has gone as follows, playing Jacoby transfers. What should you bid next?

YOU	OPPONENT	PARTNER	OPPONENT
		1NT	Pass
2♥	Pass	2♠	Pass
?			

(10) ♠ Q J 7 6 3
♥ K Q 9 4 2
♦ A
♣ 6 2

(11) ♠ K Q 6 5 4
♥ 4
♦ A Q 8 6 2
♣ A 2

(12) ♠ K 10 9 6 4 2
♥ 8 7 3 2
♦ 4 2
♣ 7

(10)_____ (11)_____ (12)_____

(10) 3♥, a forcing bid, showing five of each major.
(11) 3♦, a forcing bid, showing five spades and at least four diamonds. Even though you do have four hearts, and partner may also have four, this hand should be played in spades, since your hand is so weak. (12) Pass.

**DO NOT USE JACOBY TRANSFERS IF PARTNER'S
1NT OPENING BID IS OVERCALLED.**

Partner	RHO	You
1NT	2♦	2♥ (shows hearts, not spades).

OPENER	RESPONDER	OPENER MUST BID
1NT	4♦	4♥
OR		
1NT	4♥	4♠

You are using Jacoby and Texas transfers. What should you bid with each of these hands after partner has opened with one notrump?

(13) ♠ A Q J 8 7 2   (14) ♠ 9 8   (15) ♠ A K J 8 7 2
     ♥ 9   ♥ K Q J 7 6 5 4   ♥ 8
     ♦ 8 7 2   ♦ 8 7   ♦ K 4 3
     ♣ K 8 2   ♣ 8 3   ♣ A 10 6

(13)_____   (14)_____   (15)_____

(13) 4♠. (14) 4♦. (15) 2♥. You should then explore for a slam.

OPPONENT OPENS 1NT

BROZEL

2♣	=	Hearts and clubs
2♦	=	Hearts and diamonds
2♥	=	Hearts and spades
2♠	=	Spades plus clubs or diamonds (Partner bids 2NT to ask for minor.)
2NT	=	Clubs and diamonds

Double demands a two club bid from partner; you now bid your suit (or pass if it is clubs).

CAPPELLETTI

Double	=	Penalty
2♣	=	A one-suited hand; asks partner to bid 2♦ so you can show your suit.
2♦	=	Hearts and spades
2♥	=	Hearts plus clubs or diamonds*
2♠	=	Spades plus clubs or diamonds*
		*Partner bids 2NT to ask for your minor suit in response to 2♥ or 2♠.
2NT	=	Clubs and diamonds

LANDY

2♣	=	Hearts and spades
2NT	=	Clubs and diamonds

All other bids are natural.

Your right hand opponent has opened with one notrump. What should you do with each of the following hands?

(16) ♠ A Q J 10 8 7   (17) ♠ K J 7 4 3   (18) ♠ A Q 7 6
    ♥ 8 5   ♥ A Q 10 6 3   ♥ K J 4 2
    ♦ A 7   ♦ A   ♦ A 7 2
    ♣ 6 5 3   ♣ 9 8   ♣ 6 4

(16)_____   (17)_____   (18)_____

(16) Depends on the convention you chose: using Cappelletti, bid 2♣ followed by 2♠; using Brozel, double followed by 2♠, otherwise bid 2♠ immediately. (17) Any bid which shows the majors. (18) Pass — you do not have a long suit and would just as soon defend.

LEBENSOHL

If RHO overcalls partner's 1NT opening:

Double is for penalty.

Suit responses on the two level are signoff.

Suit responses on the three level are forcing to game.

An immediate cuebid is Stayman and game-forcing, denying a stopper in opponent's suit.

A bid of 2NT requires opener to bid 3♣ so that responder can further describe his hand:

> A three-level bid of a suit lower than opponent's is a signoff with a long suit.

> A three-level bid of a suit that previously could have been bid on the two-level is invitational.

> A delayed cuebid is Stayman and game-forcing with a stopper in opponent's suit.

An immediate bid of 3NT shows values for game without a stopper in opponent's suit.

EXAMPLE AUCTIONS USING LEBENSOHL

PARTNER	RHO	YOU	LHO	
1NT	2♥	2♠		Signoff with long spades
1NT	2♠	3♥		Game forcing with five hearts
1NT 3♣	2♠ Pass	2NT 3♥	Pass	2NT requests partner to bid 3♣. 3♥ is signoff with long hearts.
1NT 3♣	2♦ Pass	2NT 3♥	Pass	2NT requests partner to bid 3♣. 3♥ is *invitational* with long hearts since you could have signed off with 2♥ one round sooner.
1NT	2♦	3♦		Your 3♦ cuebid is Stayman, forcing to game, and denies a stopper in the opponent's suit.*
1NT 3♣	2♦ Pass	2NT 3♦	Pass	2NT asks partner to bid 3♣. Your cuebid is again Stayman and is forcing to game but this auction shows a diamond stopper.*
1NT	2♦	3NT		3NT shows the values for game but denies a stopper in diamonds.
1NT 3♣	2♦ Pass	2NT 3NT	Pass	This auction shows game values with a diamond stopper.

*You don't have the ability to distinguish between Stayman with a stopper and Stayman without a stopper if your opponent overcalls 2♣. A 3♣ bid by responder is Stayman with or without a club stopper.

You and partner have agreed to use Lebensohl after an opponent overcalls a one notrump opening bid. How do you bid with the following hands after:

PARTNER 1NT	OPPONENT 2♦	YOU ?

(19) ♠ K J 9 4
♥ Q 4 3 2
♦ 3 2
♣ A 9 2

(20) ♠ K 9 7 6
♥ A 7 5 4
♦ A 4 3
♣ 5 3

(21) ♠ A Q 9 5 3
♥ K J 9
♦ 7 4
♣ 9 4 3

(19)_____   (20)_____   (21)_____

(22) ♠ K J 9 8 3
♥ 9 6 4
♦ 9 2
♣ Q 9 3

(23) ♠ J 3 2
♥ 9 8 2
♦ 5
♣ K J 9 8 6 5

(24) ♠ A 9 4
♥ 7 4 3
♦ 3
♣ A Q J 7 6 3

(22)_____   (23)_____   (24)_____

(25) ♠ K 9 7
♥ A 7 5
♦ A 9 3
♣ J 9 7 6

(26) ♠ A Q 9
♥ Q 7 6
♦ 7 6 3
♣ K Q J 4

(27) ♠ 8 4
♥ K Q 9 7 6 2
♦ 5 3
♣ A 10 7

(25)_____   (26)_____   (27)_____

(19) 3♦. This is game-forcing Stayman and denies a diamond stopper. (20) 2NT first, then 3♦ to use Stayman and show a diamond stopper. (21) 3♠, forcing to game. (22) 2♠, signoff. (23) 2NT to force partner to bid 3♣, which you will pass. (24) 3♣, forcing to game. (25) 2NT followed by 3NT to show a diamond stopper. If the opponents are vulnerable, you might consider a penalty double. (26) 3NT, showing game values, no diamond stopper and no major. (27) 4♥.

LESSON SEVEN

Premptive Bids
Bidding After An Opponent Preempts

REASONS TO PREEMPT

Use bidding space that your opponents might need.

Accurately describe the trick-taking strength of your hand and show your long suit.

PARTNER OF THE PREEMPTER

Pass with no support or prospect of a game.

Raise with a good fit to make it more difficult for the opponents to bid.

Bid game (To make or as a sacrifice).

Bid a new suit if better place to play or for lead (Can be forcing or non-forcing, by partnership agreement).

Double if opponents make an ill-advised bid.

FOLLOW THE RULE OF TWO AND THREE

Vulnerable: Can afford a two trick set, doubled (500 points)

Not Vulnerable: Can afford a three trick set, doubled (500 points)

BIDDING OVER AN OPPONENT'S PREEMPT

OVERCALL OR DOUBLE FOR TAKEOUT (through 4♥)

If partner must bid on the 2 level = opening hand or better

If partner must bid on the 3 level or higher = 15 or more points

Double shows ability to play in unbid suits.

AFTER A TAKEOUT DOUBLE OF A PREEMPT, DOUBLER'S PARTNER SHOULD

Bid best suit. (Jump to game in a major with 10+ points)

Pass with length in the opponent's suit if this seems the best action.

CUEBID OVER TWO- AND THREE-LEVEL PREEMPTS

Michaels showing a good hand with at least 5-5 distribution

4NT OVER A PREEMPT

Over a 4♣ or 4♦ preempt, 4NT is either to play or Blackwood (by partnership agreement).

Over a 4♥ preempt, 4NT shows the minors (double is still takeout).

Over a 4♠ preempt, 4NT is takeout in the unbid suits; double is penalty.

Your right-hand opponent opened with a preemptive three heart bid. What action should you take with each of these hands?

(1) ♠ A 8 7 6
♥ J 4
♦ A Q 9
♣ 9 8 7 4

(2) ♠ A Q J 8 7 3
♥ 9
♦ A Q 9 8 7 6
♣ —

(3) ♠ K Q J 10 9 8 6
♥ 7
♦ 8 7
♣ A 10 8

(1)_____   (2)_____   (3)_____

(4) ♠ K Q 9 5
♥ 7
♦ A Q 9 6
♣ K J 10 5

(5) ♠ A K J 7 3
♥ —
♦ K Q J 7
♣ A Q J 9

(6) ♠ A 8
♥ K J 7 3
♦ K Q 8
♣ A J 10 7

(4)_____   (5)_____   (6)_____

(7) ♠ Q J 8
♥ A
♦ A K Q J 8 7 4 3
♣ 7

(8) ♠ K Q J 10 8 6
♥ 7
♦ A K Q 4
♣ 9 2

(9) ♠ A 7 3
♥ K J 9 8
♦ Q 9 7 6
♣ A 4

(7)_____   (8)_____   (9)_____

(1) Pass — you will bid strongly if partner can balance. (2) 4♣ (or cuebid 4♥ to show a good major-minor two-suiter). (3) 3♠. (4) Double. (5) Double. (6) 3NT. (7) 3NT — you are gambling that partner can stop clubs. With a heart lead, you should have nine quick tricks. It is possible that you can make six diamonds if partner has the ace of clubs and the king of spades, but the preempt has made it difficult to check on this. (8) 4♠. You need very little from partner to make game. (9) Pass. You often must pass holding both length and strength in opponent's suit.

What do you bid with each of these hands?

OPPONENT   YOU
4♠   ?

(10) ♠ A J 2
♥ A K
♦ K Q 9 7 3
♣ Q 10 3

(11) ♠ —
♥ A Q J 6 2
♦ K Q 9 4
♣ A K J 3

(12) ♠ 7
♥ A K Q 10 9 7 4 3 2
♦ 6 2
♣ 5

(10)_____   (11)_____   (12)_____

(10) Double (penalty). (11) 4NT. (12) 5♥.

LESSON EIGHT

Negative Doubles

THE NEGATIVE DOUBLE

A double of an overcall shows four cards in the unbid major(s). (By agreement can show the unbid suits).

After a one-level overcall, double promises at least 6 or 7 high card points.
(1♣ - 1♦ - Dbl or 1♣/♦ - 1♠ - Dbl)

After a two-level overcall, double promises at least 8 high card points.
(1♣ - 2♥ - Dbl)

After a three-level overcall, double promises at least 9-10 high card points.
(1♣ - 3♦ - Dbl)

Opener: Bid the limit of the combined hands assuming partner has the minimum shown by his bid.

Doubler: Bid the limit of your hand on your second opportunity to bid. Pass with a minimum.

YOU	OPPONENT	PARTNER	
1♣	1♠	Dbl.	Shows 4 hearts and possibly 4 diamonds
1♥	2♣	Dbl.	Shows 4 spades and possibly 4 diamonds
1♦	1♥	Dbl.	Shows 4 spades. Denies 5 spades; with 5 spades, bid 1♠ immediately.
1♣	1♦	Dbl.	Shows 4 hearts and 4 spades.
1♦	2♣	Dbl.	Doubler might have only one four-card major, but he must have a place to play if opener bids the wrong major.

You are playing negative doubles. What should you bid with each of these hands, after the following auction?

PARTNER	OPPONENT	YOU
1♦	1♠	?

(1) ♠ 8 7
    ♥ A Q 9 4
    ♦ 7 5 2
    ♣ K 7 5 3

(2) ♠ A 8
    ♥ 10 7 6 3
    ♦ K 7 6
    ♣ Q 8 7 4

(3) ♠ A Q 10 8 7 3
    ♥ 8 4
    ♦ 8
    ♣ 9 8 5 2

(1)_____ (2)_____ (3)_____

(4) ♠ 9 2
    ♥ A Q J 5 3
    ♦ K Q
    ♣ 10 8 6 2

(5) ♠ A J 10
    ♥ Q 7 3
    ♦ 9 6 5
    ♣ K 8 4 2

(6) ♠ 7 6
    ♥ J 5 4 2
    ♦ 9 8 3
    ♣ Q J 6 4

(4)_____ (5)_____ (6)_____

(1) Double. (2) Double. (3) Pass and hope that partner can reopen the bidding with a double. (4) 2♥. (5) 1NT. (6) Pass.

Using the negative double, what is your correct bid with each of these hands?

PARTNER	OPPONENT	YOU
1♣	1♦	?

(7) ♠ A Q 6 2
    ♥ 9 5 4 3
    ♦ Q 3 2
    ♣ 5 4

(8) ♠ A 7 6 3
    ♥ 10 8
    ♦ 3 2
    ♣ K Q 7 6 4

(9) ♠ K J 6 5 4
    ♥ K 9 8
    ♦ 3
    ♣ K 8 7 2

(7)_____ (8)_____ (9)_____

(7) Double. (8) 1♠; double would show four hearts and four spades. (9) 1♠.

38

You are using negative doubles. What should you bid with each of the following hands after the bidding has gone:

YOU	OPPONENT	PARTNER	OPPONENT
1♣	1♠	Dbl.	Pass
?			

(10) ♠ 8 7
   ♥ K J 7 4
   ♦ A 8 3
   ♣ A J 9 8

(11) ♠ A J 10
   ♥ Q 5
   ♦ K 7 2
   ♣ K 10 7 4 3

(12) ♠ Q 4
   ♥ A 9 6
   ♦ 9 4 3
   ♣ A Q J 9 3

(10)_____   (11)_____   (12)_____

(13) ♠ A 7
   ♥ K Q J 6
   ♦ 9 3
   ♣ A J 7 4 2

(14) ♠ 9
   ♥ A Q J 7
   ♦ K Q 7
   ♣ A Q 7 5 2

(15) ♠ A Q J 10
   ♥ 9 3
   ♦ K Q 8
   ♣ A Q J 4

(13)_____   (14)_____   (15)_____

(10) 2♥. (11) 1NT. (12) 2♣. (13) 3♥. (14) 4♥. (15) Pass if the opponents are vulnerable. If not, you can either pass or bid 2NT.

Using negative doubles, what is your proper bid after the following sequence?

PARTNER	OPPONENT	YOU	OPPONENT
1♣	1♠	Dbl.	Pass
2♥	Pass	?	

(16) ♠ 8 4
   ♥ A Q J 8
   ♦ 9 8 7 2
   ♣ Q 9 5

(17) ♠ K 7
   ♥ A 8 4 3
   ♦ 8 3 2
   ♣ K 8 7 5

(18) ♠ A Q
   ♥ K J 7 2
   ♦ K Q 7 5
   ♣ 8 7 3

(16)_____   (17)_____   (18)_____

(16) Pass. (17) 3♥. (18) 4♥ — if partner had made any other bid, you would have bid game in notrump.

LESSON NINE

Limit Raises – Splinter Bids
Strong Major Suit Raises

RAISES IN PARTNER'S MAJOR SUIT

LIMIT RAISES

Single jump $\begin{cases} \text{10-12 points} \\ \text{Four-card trump support} \end{cases}$

*THREE NOTRUMP = Strong Major Raise (13 to 15 points)

Shows balanced distribution with at least four trumps.
Forcing to game in partner's suit.

OPENER	RESPONDER
1♠	3NT

*Some players use 2NT as a strong major suit raise
(see page 45)

SPLINTER BID BY RESPONDER

A double jump shift showing a singleton or void in suit
bid, plus four-card support for partner's major and at least
13 points. Forcing to game in partner's suit.

OPENER		RESPONDER
1♥		4♦
	OR	
1♠		4♣
	OR	
1♥		3♠

You are using limit raises, splinter bids and three notrump as a strong major raise. What should you bid with each of these hands after partner has opened one heart and right hand opponent has passed?

(1) ♠ A Q
    ♥ K 7 6 4
    ♦ 9 7 6 5 2
    ♣ 8 7

(2) ♠ 8 7
    ♥ A 8 7 2
    ♦ K Q 8 7 4
    ♣ 7 3

(3) ♠ 9 4 3
    ♥ Q 10 9 8
    ♦ 9 8 3
    ♣ A Q 8

(1)_____

(2)_____

(3)_____

(4) ♠ A 7
    ♥ K J 7 2
    ♦ A J 7 4
    ♣ 5 4 3

(5) ♠ 9 2
    ♥ K 8 4 3
    ♦ A K Q 5 3
    ♣ 8 6

(6) ♠ A Q 8
    ♥ 9 8
    ♦ K Q 6 3
    ♣ Q 5 3 2

(4)_____

(5)_____

(6)_____

(7) ♠ A 8 7 3
    ♥ K 6 4 3
    ♦ 8
    ♣ A Q 5 4

(8) ♠ 7 5
    ♥ K Q
    ♦ A K Q 7 5 3
    ♣ A 7 5

(9) ♠ 6
    ♥ A 7 5 4
    ♦ K Q J 4
    ♣ A 9 7 4

(7)_____

(8)_____

(9)_____

(1) 3♥. (2) 3♦. (3) 2♥. (4) 3NT. (5) 2♦. Show your strong diamond suit and then bid game in hearts. With the proper controls in the unbid suits, partner can consider a slam. (6) 2NT. (7) 4♦. (8) 3♦. (9) 3♣.

41

Using splinter bids in the sequence shown, what would you bid with each of the following hands?

YOU	OPPONENT	PARTNER	OPPONENT
1♠	Pass	4♦	Pass
?			

(10) ♠ A K 8 7 3
    ♥ Q 7 6 5
    ♦ K 7
    ♣ 3 2

(11) ♠ K 9 8 7 5 4
    ♥ A Q J
    ♦ 7 6
    ♣ A Q

(12) ♠ K Q 8 7 4
    ♥ A Q
    ♦ A 7 5 2
    ♣ 8 3

(10)_____ (11)_____ (12)_____

(10) 4♣. (11) 4NT — if partner has two aces and two kings, you should be able to make a grand slam. (12) 4♥. If partner has the club ace or king, you should be able to make a slam. But it is possible for your partnership to have everything but the two high clubs. Blackwood won't tell you if this is so.

Partner's three notrump response shows the equivalent of a forcing heart raise. What should you do next with each of these hands?

YOU	OPPONENT	PARTNER	OPPONENT
1♥	Pass	3NT	Pass
?			

(13) ♠ A K
    ♥ K Q 8 7 5 3
    ♦ 8 7 2
    ♣ 8 5

(14) ♠ K 7
    ♥ A 7 6 5 3
    ♦ K Q J 5
    ♣ A 8

(15) ♠ 7 5
    ♥ A Q 8 7 5
    ♦ A Q 8
    ♣ K Q 7

(13)_____ (14)_____ (15)_____

(13) 4♥. (14) 4NT (Blackwood). (15) 4♦ — if partner has control of spades there should be a slam.

After you open the bidding with one spade, partner responds with a limit raise of three spades. What should you rebid with each of these hands?

(16) ♠ A 8 7 5 2
 ♥ A K 8
 ♦ 8 5
 ♣ J 3 2

(17) ♠ K Q 8 7 6
 ♥ 8 7
 ♦ A K 9
 ♣ K 4 2

(18) ♠ K J 9 8 7 3
 ♥ A 8
 ♦ K 7
 ♣ A K Q

(16)_____

(17)_____

(18)_____

(16) Pass. (17) 4♣. (18) 4NT (Blackwood) — if partner has an ace you will bid six spades; if he has two aces and a king, you can bid seven.

Playing splinter bids, what should you bid with each of these hands? The bidding has gone:

YOU	OPPONENT	PARTNER	OPPONENT
		1♠	Pass
4♦	Pass	4♥	Pass
?			

(19) ♠ K 7 6 4 2
 ♥ 9 3
 ♦ 2
 ♣ A K Q J 5

(20) ♠ A Q 8 3
 ♥ K 9 8
 ♦ 6
 ♣ K J 9 8 7

(21) ♠ K J 8 7 3
 ♥ K Q J 10 9
 ♦ —
 ♣ Q 3 2

(19)_____

(20)_____

(21)_____

(19) 4NT. (20) 4NT. (21) 5♦, showing a void.

SPLINTER BY OPENER

A double jump shift guarantees game in partner's suit.
Shows a singleton or void in the suit bid.

OPENER	RESPONDER
1♦	1♥
4♣*	

*Shows four hearts and
a singleton or void in clubs.

♠ A x x
♥ K Q J x
♦ A K J x x
♣ x

In the following sequence, partner's four club bid shows a singleton club with four card spade support. What should you bid next?

PARTNER	OPPONENT	YOU	OPPONENT
1♦	Pass	1♠	Pass
4♣	Pass	?	

(22) ♠ A Q 7 6 4	(23) ♠ K 8 7 5	(24) ♠ A K Q 8
♥ 8 7 3	♥ 8 7	♥ 9
♦ 7 2	♦ K 9 3	♦ K Q J 8 5
♣ 8 7 5	♣ Q J 9 3	♣ 8 7 3

(22)_____   (23)_____   (24)_____

(22) 4♠. (23) 4♠ (your club values are useless). (24) 4NT (Blackwood). If partner has two aces (or shows one ace with a club void) you should be able to make a slam.

JACOBY 2NT = A STRONG MAJOR RAISE

TWO NOTRUMP = strong major suit raise
(at least 13 points)
Shows semi-balanced distribution
with at least four trumps.
Forcing to game in partner's suit.

OPENER	RESPONDER
1♥/1♠	2NT

OPENER'S REBIDS AFTER RESPONDER BIDS 2NT

(1) Bid a singleton or void at the three level.

OPENER	RESPONDER
1♠	2NT
3♦ (shows a diamond singleton or void)	

(2) Bid a second good five-card suit at the four level.

OPENER	RESPONDER
1♥	2NT
4♣ (shows five good clubs)	

(3) With neither of the above, show point count:

4 of agreed major	= a dead-minimum opening bid with no slam interest
3NT	= a little extra strength (about 15-17 points)
3 of agreed major	= 18+ points

After hearing opener's rebid, responder should be able to decide whether to sign off in game or to look for slam.

LESSON TEN

Grand Slam Force
Interference Over Blackwood

GRAND SLAM FORCE

Jump to 5NT asks for 2 of top 3 honors in the agreed trump suit. (If no suit has been agreed upon it asks for honors in the suit bid last.)

Responses {
With 2 of top 3 honors bid grand slam
With 0 or 1, bid small slam

After Blackwood 4NT, a bid of 6♣ becomes Grand Slam Force (provided clubs is not the trump suit).

You are using the Grand Slam Force convention. What should you bid with each of these hands after the bidding has gone:

YOU	PARTNER
1♠	3NT (strong major raise)
?	

(1)   ♠ K Q 8 7 2
      ♥ A 10 9
      ♦ K Q J
      ♣ A 10

(2)   ♠ Q J 8 7 3
      ♥ A K 7
      ♦ A K J 8 3
      ♣ —

(3)   ♠ A 8 7 5 2
      ♥ A K 9
      ♦ —
      ♣ A K Q 7 4

(1)_____   (2)_____   (3)_____

(1) 4NT (Blackwood). (2) 5NT. (3) 5NT.

You are using the Grand Slam Force convention. What should you bid with each of these hands after the bidding has gone:

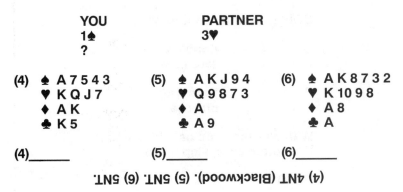

	YOU	PARTNER
	1♠	3♥
	?	

(4)
♠ A 7 5 4 3
♥ K Q J 7
♦ A K
♣ K 5

(5)
♠ A K J 9 4
♥ Q 9 8 7 3
♦ A
♣ A 9

(6)
♠ A K 8 7 3 2
♥ K 10 9 8
♦ A 8
♣ A

(4)_____   (5)_____   (6)_____

(4) 4NT (Blackwood). (5) 5NT. (6) 5NT.

Using the Grand Slam Force, what is your next bid in this sequence?

	YOU	PARTNER
	1♠	3NT (strong major raise)
	4NT	5♦
	?	

(7)
♠ A 8 5 3 2
♥ K 8
♦ A Q 8
♣ K Q 5

(8)
♠ A 9 7 4 3
♥ K 9
♦ A K Q 7 4
♣ A

(9)
♠ K 8 7 3 2
♥ A K Q 7 5
♦ A
♣ A 9

(7)_____   (8)_____   (9)_____

(7) 6♣. (8) 6♣. (9) 6♣.

47

BIDDING OVER BLACKWOOD INTERFERENCE

DOPI (pronounced dopey)

D	=	double with
O	=	zero aces

P	=	pass with
I	=	one ace

With two aces, bid next higher suit.
With three aces, skip a suit.

DEPO

D	=	double with
E	=	even number of aces (0, 2, 4)

P	=	pass with
O	=	odd number of aces (1 or 3)

Your partnership has to decide when to use DOPI and when to use DEPO. Many partnerships use DOPI when the interference is below five of their agreed suit and DEPO when the interference is above five of their agreed suit.

In all the following sequences, you are using DOPI after interference with Blackwood. What do you bid in each case?

PARTNER	OPPONENT	YOU	OPPONENT
1♠	Pass	3♠*	4♥
4NT	5♥	?	
			*limit raise

(10) ♠ K Q 8 7
    ♥ A 6
    ♦ 9 8 6 4
    ♣ Q 7 6

(11) ♠ K Q 8 7
    ♥ 8 6
    ♦ K Q J
    ♣ 6 5 3 2

(12) ♠ A 8 7 5
    ♥ 9 5 4
    ♦ A Q 8 7
    ♣ 8 5

(10)_____

(11)_____

(12)_____

(10) Pass. (11) Double. (12) 5♠.

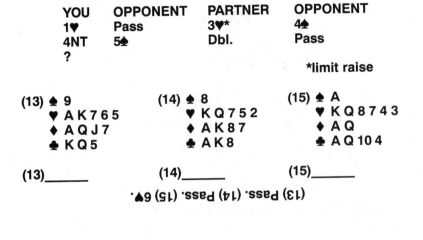

YOU	OPPONENT	PARTNER	OPPONENT
1♥	Pass	3♥*	4♠
4NT	5♠	Dbl.	Pass
?			
			*limit raise

(13) ♠ 9
♥ A K 7 6 5
♦ A Q J 7
♣ K Q 5

(14) ♠ 8
♥ K Q 7 5 2
♦ A K 8 7
♣ A K 8

(15) ♠ A
♥ K Q 8 7 4 3
♦ A Q
♣ A Q 10 4

(13)_____   (14)_____   (15)_____

(13) Pass. (14) Pass. (15) 6♥.

YOU	OPPONENT	PARTNER	OPPONENT
1♥	Pass	3♥*	4♠
4NT	5♠	Pass	Pass
?			
			*limit raise

(16) ♠ 9
♥ A K 7 6 5
♦ A Q J 7
♣ K Q 5

(17) ♠ A
♥ K Q J 10 9
♦ K Q 7 6 4
♣ K 7

(18) ♠ A
♥ K Q 8 7 5 3
♦ A Q 6
♣ A Q 8

(16)_____   (17)_____   (18)_____

(16) 6♥. (17) Double; you are missing two aces. (18) 6♥. (You could ask for kings, but even if partner has two, the grand slam may still rely on a finesse.)

PART II

DUPLICATE BRIDGE

Differences Between
Duplicate Bridge and Rubber Bridge

1. Each hand is dealt only once at a session and then remains intact, being played at each table in turn.

2. Each hand is scored as an entity, with no relationship to preceding or following hands. There is a bonus of 50 points for making a partscore, 300 points for making a non-vulnerable game, and 500 points for making a vulnerable game. The penalty for not making a contract is the same as in rubber bridge. No bonus is awarded for honors.

3. The dealer and vulnerability are indicated on the duplicate board, which is used to move the cards from table to table.

4. Each pair competes against all the other players who are sitting in the same direction by trying to gain more points or lose fewer points on each hand.

5. Since duplicate bridge is purely a game of comparative scores, the players constantly try to make an extra trick when playing the hand, even occasionally jeopardizing an easy game. They play in notrump instead of a minor suit just for the extra points involved. They play in two spades down one for a loss of 100 points, when the opponents can make two hearts for 110. All this requires close judgment and greatly improves accuracy in bidding and play.

6. Sacrifice bidding is very important – if the opponents can make 620 points for their game, a sacrifice which loses only 500 points is a very good score. Vulnerability must be closely watched – sacrifice bidding is normally taboo at unfavorable vulnerability, while under the opposite circumstances a sacrifice can often be extremely profitable. Sacrificing against slams follows the same pattern – going down as many as six tricks not vulnerable for 1400 points produces a good result when the opponents can score 1430 for a small slam. But be very sure they will make it – nothing produces a worse result than sacrificing against a game or slam which is destined to fail.

DUPLICATE SCORING

POINTS PER TRICK

Notrump { 1st trick 40 / Each add'l 30

Spades and Hearts 30

Diamonds and Clubs 20

OVERTRICKS

Not Doubled: Trick points only

Doubled Overtricks (each)
Not vul.: 100   Vul.: 200

Redoubled Overtricks (each)
Not vul.: 200   Vul.: 400

BONUSES

Game { Not vulnerable 300 / Vulnerable 500

Partscore 50

Making doubled contract 50
Making redbld contract 100

Small Slam { Not vul. 500 / Vul. 750

Grand Slam { Not. vul. 1000 / Vul. 1500

PENALTIES

(Points per trick short of contract)

	Not vulnerable			Vulnerable		
	Undbld	Dbld	Redbld	Undbld	Dbld	Redbld
1st undertrick	50	100	200	100	200	400
2nd and 3rd	50	200	400	100	300	600
Each addl.	50	300	600	100	300	600

Here are some possible results – what is the correct score for each, using duplicate scoring?

	Not Vulnerable	Vulnerable		Not Vulnerable	Vulnerable
1NT+1	(1) _____	(2) _____	1D+3	(15) _____	(16) _____
1NT+2	(3) _____	(4) _____	5C+1	(17) _____	(18) _____
4S-1	(5) _____	(6) _____	3H-2	(19) _____	(20) _____
$3H^x$	(7) _____	(8) _____	$4S^x$-1	(21) _____	(22) _____
4H+1	(9) _____	(10) _____	7C	(23) _____	(24) _____
2C	(11) _____	(12) _____	7NT	(25) _____	(26) _____
$6NT^x$-2	(13) _____	(14) _____	5S-2	(27) _____	(28) _____

(1) 120. (2) 120. (3) 150. (4) 150. (5) 50. (6) 100. (7) 530. (8) 730. (9) 450. (10) 650. (11) 90. (12) 90. (13) 300. (14) 500. (15) 130. (16) 130. (17) 420. (18) 620. (19) 100. (20) 200. (21) 100. (22) 200. (23) 1440. (24) 2140. (25) 1520. (26) 2220. (27) 100. (28) 200.

THE DUPLICATE BOARD

To start a duplicate game, the director puts several boards on each table. Unless he specifies otherwise, the players should shuffle the cards and replace them in their slots. Then each player removes his own cards from the lowest-numbered board and bids them just as in rubber bridge. But there is a difference when it comes to the play of the hand. Instead of putting all four cards in the center of the table, each player merely places the card which he wishes to play face up in front of himself. When it is dummy's turn to play, declarer instructs dummy which card to play, and dummy picks it up and moves it toward himself. After all four cards are played, they are turned over, still in front of each player. The short side of the card points toward the side that won the trick – see the illustration below. North-South have won ten tricks, East-West have won three.

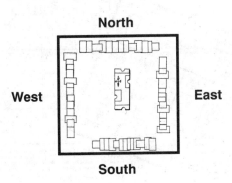

The director will provide a traveling score for each board in play, such as the one illustrated below. It is North's responsibility to fill out the traveling score after each hand, entering on the line opposite his pair number the opponents' number, the contract, the number of tricks (or undertricks) made and the score, either in the North-South column if North-South achieved a plus score, or in the East-West column if East-West were plus. Each player should check to be sure that North has entered the correct score. Instead of using travelers, some games and tournaments use pick-up slips to record the results of the hands. Pick-up slips allow the director to get a head start on scoring the game, but players are not able to compare their results with those of the other players during the game.

The final scoring process, after all the hands for the session have been played, is called matchpointing. Basically, a pair receives one point for each other pair they beat on a board, and one-half point for each pair they tie. Therefore, the worst pair on each hand receives zero points, since they did not beat anyone, while the best pair receives one less point than the number of times the board is played, since they beat every other pair except themselves.

OFFICIAL (Mitchell or Howell) TRAVELING SCORE

Bid, play and score this board without comment and proceed immediately to the next.

NORTH PLAYER only keeps score

ENTER PAIR NO. OF E-W PAIR   Board No. 1

N-S Pair	E-W Pair	CON-TRACT	By	MADE	DOWN	FINAL SCORE North South	East West	E-W Match Points	N-S Match Points
1	1	2D	5	2		90			3X
2	3	4D	S	1			50		X
	5	2H	E		1	50			2
	7	1N	N	1		90			3X
2		1N	N	1			50		X
	4	3H×	E		2	300			6
		3D	S	3		110			5
								1	2X	21
								2	5X	
								3	5X	
								4	O	
								5	4	
								6	1	
								7	2X	21

...lge in post-mortems; if you must, only at end of round. Play congenially. Announce or display private conventions. Refrain from giving lessons, especially to opponents. Do not make your own rulings; call your game director, that's his job. Count your cards before and after.

BARON/BARCLAY BRIDGE SUPPLIES
1-800-274-2221   #7274

Form 6235

E-W PAIR

BARON BARCLAY BRIDGE SUPPLIES

ALL DEALS PLAYED THIS ROUND WILL BE SCORED ON THIS CARD. CIRCLE DIRECTION OF DECLARER.

E-W OK   RB

E-W SCORE

N-S PAIR   1

| N-S PAIR | MADE | DOWN | BOARD NUMBER | N-S CONTRACT | E-W CONTRACT | E-W | WON | DOWN | E-W SCORE |

N-S SCORE	420	4	45	1	E W		100
		1	3N	2	E W	2H 3	140
	420		3N	3	N S		

USE BOTTOM HALF FIRST – TEAR AT PERFORATION

Here are the scores made on a board in an 11-table duplicate game. Try your hand at entering the scores and matchpointing them. In matchpoints an x or a - after a score is used to indicate one-half point. (See page 57 for answers).

(EW vulnerable)

NS #1 vs. EW #10
S bid 3S, made 10 tricks

NS #2 vs. EW #1
N bid 4S, made 10 tricks

NS #3 vs. EW #3
S bid 4S, made 9 tricks

NS #4 vs. EW #5
W bid 5C doubled, made
   9 tricks

NS #5 vs. EW #7
S bid 4S, made 10 tricks

NS #6 vs. EW #9
W bid 3 C, made 9 tricks

NS #7 vs. EW #11
N bid 3NT, made 9 tricks

NS #8 vs. EW #2
N bid 3NT, made 10 tricks

NS #9 vs. EW #4
S bid 3NT, made 9 tricks

NS #10 vs. EW #6
S bid 3NT, made 8 tricks

NS #11 vs. EW #8
S bid 3NT, made 9 tricks

FOR REVIEW —
ABBREVIATIONS FOR SCORING

Notrump	— **NT**	**North**	— **N**	**Double**	— **x**
Spades	— **S**	**East**	— **E**	**Redouble**	— **xx**
Hearts	— **H**	**South**	— **S**		
Diamonds	— **D**	**West**	— **W**		
Clubs	— **C**				

OFFICIAL (Mitchell or Howell) TRAVELING SCORE

Bid, Play & Score this board without comment and Proceed immediately to the next.

NORTH PLAYER only keeps score

SECTION _____ ENTER PAIR NO. OF EW PAIR   Board No. _____

N-S Pair No.	CON-TRACT	BY	Made	Down	SCORE N-S	SCORE E-W	E-W Pair No.	Match Points
1								
2								
3								
4								
5								
6								
7								
8								
9								
10								
11								
12								
13							1	
14							2	
15							3	
16							4	
17							5	
18							6	
19							7	
20							8	
21							9	
22							10	
23							11	
24							12	

OFFICIAL (Mitchell or Howell) TRAVELING SCORE

Bid, Play & Score this board without comment and Proceed immediately to the next.

NORTH PLAYER only keeps score

SECTION _____ ENTER PAIR NO. OF EW PAIR   Board No. **6**

N-S Pair No.	CON-TRACT	BY	Made	Down	SCORE N-S	SCORE E-W	E-W Pair No.	Match Points
1	3 S	S	4		170		10	3
2	4 S	N	4		420		1	7 x
3	4 S	S		1		50	3	1 x
4	5 c x	W	2		500		5	10
5	4 S	S	4		420		7	7 x
6	3 c	W	3			110	9	0
7	3 NT	N	3		400		11	5
8	3 NT	N	4		430		2	9
9	3 NT	S	3		400		4	5
10	3 NT	S		1		50	6	1 x
11	3 NT	S	3		400		8	5
12								55
13							1	2 x
14							2	1
15							3	8 x
16							4	5
17							5	0
18							6	8 x
19							7	2 x
20							8	5
21							9	10
22							10	7
23							11	5
24							12	55

THE RECAPITULATION SHEET

After the hands are all matchpointed the results are copied onto a recapitulation sheet (commonly called a "recap").

Pair No.	Names	Rank	Total Points	1	2	3	4	5	6	7	8	9	10	11	12	13	14	15
1	Lee + Bob Mendelsohn	①	124	4	3	6	7	7	6	6	2	4	2	7	4	1	5	4
2	B. Cagan - G. Baldwin	2	120	3	5	5	4	1	8	4	3	1	8	4	8	2	7	5
3	Roy and Jane Hill		103	6.	5	0	8	5	1	5	1	8	0	4	2	0	6	3
4	H. + S. Silverman	3/4	112.	6.	2	3.	3	0	5	3	8	3	7	8	1	7	4	
5	Dr. and Mrs. M. Colmer		95	8	0	3.	2	6	2	0	7	2	1	4	0	8	3	
6	K. Bailey - H. Fein	3/4	112.	5	5	6	5.	2	0	8	0	7	6	6	3	6		
7	R. Goldwater - G. Weiss		104	1	1	1	0	8	7	7	6	0	5	2	5	5		
8	Mr. + Mrs. R. Hewitt		106	1	7	6	1	4	3	1	4	6	4	1	6			
9	P. Mitchell - R. Oshlag		95	1	8	2	5.	3	4	2	5	5	3	0				
10			972															
11																		

THE CONVENTION CARD

One side of the card is used to keep track of the score for the session. Write down each contract as soon as the bidding is over – this prevents misunderstandings. After the deal is completed, check to be sure that North entered the correct score on the traveler or pick-up slip – everyone makes mistakes from time to time. Enter your own score on your convention card.

The other side of the card is more complicated. Basically, you are trying to summarize your bidding system so that the opponents can tell what your bids mean – they are entitled to as much information as your partner possesses; it is contrary to both to the spirit and to the laws of bridge to have secret under-standings with partner concerning bids and plays.

Take something as common as an opening notrump bid. Most Americans open one notrump with something in the neighbor-

CONVENTION CARD

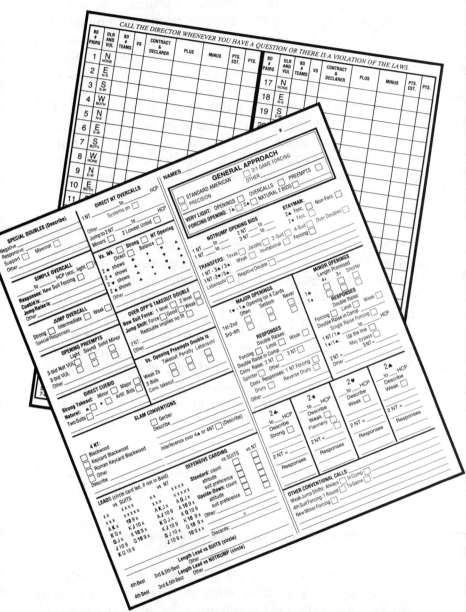

Note that there are several kinds of convention cards in use throughout North America, so the one you fill out may be slightly different than the above sample.

hood of 15 to 17 high card points. However, if you were playing in Great Britain you might find that more than half of the players use 12 to 14 points as their opening notrump range. They also frequently open four card majors, while a great number of Americans prefer five card majors. You certainly have the right to play weak or strong notrump, four or five card majors, but your opponents must know what you are doing.

Put your name and your partner's name on the card. Then indicate your bidding system – most of us play Standard American. Go over the balance of the card with your partner; it will help to clear up some sources of misunderstanding. If you play only the basic conventions, just check the boxes which apply.

ALERTING

If you have checked any red boxes, or written in any special conventions on the card, you and your partner are obligated to warn the opponents of this, directly after the bid is made. The proper procedure is for the partner of the bidder to say "Alert" before his right hand opponent bids. Then the opponent whose turn it is has the right to ask what the bid means. (The other opponent may ask at his turn to bid.) Note that **partner** of the bidder does the explaining. Similarly, when the opponents alert you to an unusual bid, you and your partner have the right to request an explanation, either at your first turn to bid or at any subsequent turn, or at any time during the play of the hand when it is the questioner's turn to play. You may also ask before you make the opening lead. If partner is on lead you may ask after the dummy is tabled but before you play to the first trick. An explanation of the alert procedure and a list of alertable bids is available at duplicate clubs.

THE LAWS OF DUPLICATE BRIDGE

This little book contains the guidelines of duplicate bridge and is carried by all directors. When there is an infraction of the rules, any player (except the dummy) may call the director for a ruling, which is basically designed to restore the equities at the table. All players should be familiar with the laws, since they govern the conduct of the game. When the director makes a ruling, he will normally read the appropriate law from the book — if he does not, any player may ask to see the book and read it for himself. DO NOT ATTEMPT TO MAKE RULINGS YOUR-SELF AND DO NOT PERMIT ANY PLAYER AT THE TABLE TO DO SO — this is what the director is for.

WHEN TO CALL THE DIRECTOR

It is not bad manners to call the director when in doubt — he is always very happy to keep the game running smoothly. The director MUST be called if any of the following occur:

1. A revoke
2. Bid or pass out of turn
3. Insufficient bid
4. Lead out of turn
5. Undue hesitation
6. Failure to alert

RIGHTS AND RESPONSIBILITIES
OF THE DUMMY

The dummy may:

**Point out a revoke <u>after</u> the
hand has been played.
Ask declarer to double-check
if he fails to follow suit.
Warn partner if he is about
to lead from the wrong hand.**

The dummy may NOT:

**Call the director.
Play a card except at
declarer's request.
Look at partner's hand.
Comment on bidding or play
before hand is over.**

To Summarize — THE DUMMY SHOULD ATTEMPT TO PREVENT AN INFRACTION OF THE RULES, BUT MAY TAKE NO FURTHER PART IN THE PLAY OF THE HAND ONCE THE AUCTION IS OVER.

THE SKIP BID WARNING

Under duplicate rules, a player who makes a bid which skips a level (any opening bid above the one level, any overcall which is one or more levels higher than necessary, or any response or rebid on a level higher than required) is permitted to announce "I am about to make a skip bid, please hesitate ten seconds." This warning permits the next player to consider his possible alternatives without giving undue information to partner. Without a skip bid warning, passing quickly could announce that he holds few cards of value, while passing slowly could say "Partner, I have close to a bid." If no skip bid warning is given then there is less chance for redress if there is either a "fast" bid or a prolonged hesitation. You must either use the skip bid warning *every* time you make a skip bid or not at all. (You cannot just use it for strong skip bids or weak ones).

HESITATIONS

In a crucial situation, everyone is entitled to have enough time to consider all the possible alternatives. However, it is incumbent upon partner not to place undue significance upon the hesitation and to bid only the cards which he can see. If you have hesitated unduly and are on the borderline of a bid, it is better to make the bid and take the pressure off partner. The opponents have the right to call the director when there is a long pause and then a pass, to protect both you and them against your partner taking advantage of your long thought. Naturally, your side has the same right — whenever there is an unnecessarily long pause at a crucial spot be sure to call the director immediately, just to be certain that everyone is protected.

THE AMERICAN CONTRACT BRIDGE LEAGUE

Organized duplicate bridge in the United States, Canada, Mexico, Bermuda and certain U.S. outposts overseas is governed by the American Contract Bridge League.

The basic unit of the ACBL is the sanctioned duplicate club, which might hold many sessions a week or meet infrequently. Above the local club is the Unit, which is authorized to run both single games and multiple events lasting over a weekend or longer. When you join the ACBL, you also join your local Unit and they receive a share of your dues. Your club director will handle your application or direct you to the proper person; applications may also be sent directly to the ACBL at 2990 Airways Boulevard, Memphis, TN 38116-3847.

Units are grouped into Districts for the purpose of holding larger tournaments, with larger awards. The largest tournaments of all are the North American Bridge Championships, which are held three times a year, in various cities.

WHY JOIN THE ACBL?

The goal of all serious duplicate bridge players is to win Master Points. These are awarded by all sanctioned clubs, at Unit and District events, and at North American Bridge Championships. By winning various combinations of points in different events a player progresses from being a brand new Rookie member, to becoming a Junior Master with five points, through a series of steps to the goal of Life Master with 300 or more points, a number of which must be won at Sectional, District and National events. For a complete explanation of the Master Point system, ask your club director for a copy of *Adventures in Duplicate*, published by the ACBL.

RECOMMENDED BOOKS FOR BEGINNERS

Blackwood, Easley & Hanson, Keith:
  Card Play Fundamentals #0530 .... $6.95
Goodwin, Jude: Teach Me to Play #3160 .... $12.95
Kantar, Eddie:
  Introduction to Declarer's Play #2130 .... $7.00
Kantar, Eddie:
  Introduction to Defender's Play #2135 .... $10.00
Lampert, Harry:
  The Fun Way to Serious Bridge #3230 .... $10.00
Stewart, Frank & Baron, Randy:
  The Bridge Book, Vol. 1 #0101 .... $9.95
Penick, Mike:
  Beginning Bridge Complete #0660 .... $9.95

RECOMMENDED BOOKS FOR INTERMEDIATE PLAYERS

Hardy, Max & Bruno, Steve: 2 Over 1
  Game Force: An Introduction #4750 .... $9.95
Kaplan, Edgar: Competitive Bidding #2165 .... $7.00
Kelsey, Hugh:
  Countdown to Better Bridge #0620 .... $9.95
Lampert, Harry:
  The Fun Way to Advanced Bridge #0575 .... $11.95
Lawrence, Mike: Hand Evaluation #1772 .... $11.95
Root, William: Commonsense Bidding #3015 .... $15.00